Cracking the Home Seller's Code:

The Secret Combination to Unlocking Your Home's Maximum Value

Brian Ernst

ISBN-13: 978-1-950710-11-9 (Amazon Print)
ISBN-13: 978-1-950710-12-6 (Ingram Spark) Paperback
ISBN-13: 978-1-950710-13-3 (Ingram Spark) Hardcover
ISBN-13: 978-1-950710-14-0 (Smashwords)

For bulk purchase and for booking, contact:

Brian Ernst
brian@brianernst.net

2970 Peachtree Circle
Aurora, IL 60502
(630) 730-0838

Table of Contents

Introduction

Thank you and congratulations on purchasing this book, *Cracking The Home Seller's Code: The Secret Combination to Unlocking Your Home's Maximum Value.* I have written this book to provide you with information about how to sell your home for maximum value as quickly as possible.

In my career as a real estate agent, I have worked with many sellers. One of the things that I noticed is that they all have a common set of questions that they routinely ask. However, I have also come to realize that most of these questions are not really the *best* questions they should ask. In other words, they are asking a lot of good questions, but they could be asking even better ones. When you ask the best questions possible, you will receive the best and most useful answers possible.

So, what do you think happens when you ask average or bad questions?

For example, most sellers ask me, "What is the value of my home, and how much commission will you charge me?" If you ask bad questions such as these, you may end up listing your home with an agent who says they will sell your home at the highest price and charge you the lowest commission. This doesn't ensure that your home will be sold any time soon. In fact, there are incompetent and unscrupulous agents out there who will simply list your home, use it to pick up buyer leads, and make money off your sign and advertisements. They may be selling other homes, but they aren't selling your overpriced one.

The questions you should really be asking are "How much money am I going to walk away with, and are you the right agent for the job?" That's why I decided to write this book. I want to use my expertise to help you ask the best questions possible so that you can actually sell your home for the best price possible.

You see, it's not just about pricing and commissions. I want to teach you how the process works and what the best practices are when it comes to selling your property. I'm going to show you how to prepare your home for sale and what to do to market it. You will also learn how appraisals work, how homes are listed, and where to find the best real estate agent. I want to help you change your mindset so that you can get maximum value for your property quickly and with as minimal inconvenience as possible.

After decades in this line of work, I understand just how stressful and frustrating it can be for home sellers. I've seen too many sellers overprice their homes and end up with few or no offers. I have seen people blow a deal because they focused too much on the wrong principles instead of selling their home. By the time you are through with this book, you will understand that home selling has more to do with people than homes. My experience has taught me how to relate to people's needs and how to find solutions to their challenges.

So, what are you waiting for?

This book will help paint a clearer picture on how to sell your home without the stress and pain. You will see just how easy, efficient, and cost-effective the process can be if you simply follow the right steps. The content in this book is easy to follow so that you can elevate yourself from basic knowledge to more advanced real estate wisdom. I want you to graduate from Real Estate 101 and move to Real Estate 201.

I encourage you to make the decision to invest in this book right now. It will definitely save you a lot of time, money, and frustration as you sell your home.

Are you ready to begin this journey?

Let's go!

Chapter One

Determining the Value of Your Home

One of the things issues that all home sellers focus on is the value of their properties. Indeed, this is a key consideration because you want to get the best price possible for your home. If you were to ask most real estate agents to estimate the value of your home, they would point to certain factors, such as the market value of your property relative to similar properties. They would base their answer on which properties are selling like hotcakes and which ones aren't doing so well in your area, your local market.

However, from my professional experience, I know that this is the wrong approach. The reason is that you, the seller, are asking the wrong question. Instead of asking "What is my home worth?" you should ask, "How much money am I going to take away once the home has been sold?" Now, don't get me wrong here. Determining what your home is worth is very important, but what you end up with is even more critical. There's a huge difference in altering your perspective, and here's why:

Asking the Right Questions

You need to understand that the value of your home is dependent on market conditions that are beyond your control. However, what you end up putting in your pocket (which is what you should *really* care about!) is dependent on you. In other words, there are things that you can do to ensure that you walk away with a lot more money, regardless of the perceived value of your home.

So, what are some of these factors that determine how much money you pocket as a seller?

1. **Closing costs.** How much are the closing costs of the deal?

2. **Payment of the closing costs.** Who will be paying for the costs? How will the costs be paid?

3. **Condition of your property.** What physical shape is your home in? Are there any upgrades or updates that you have done to your home?

4. **Current market conditions.** Are there many buyers in the market right now who are actively searching for a new home? How many homes are actively on sale or have been sold?

5. **Average market time-out.** How much time, on average, does it take a property to be sold?

6. **Economic factors.** Are there any economic influencers that are encouraging/discouraging buyers to purchase homes? For example, there are instances when first-time homebuyers can access lines of credit. If such incentives are no longer available, then market demand for homes can completely plummet.

As you can see, there are specific factors that are within your control and others that are not. By asking the right questions, you get to learn and understand how to get the most value for your property. Another thing you should understand is that there are many variables that come into play when estimating how much money you are going to make. So, if someone tries to tell you exactly what your home is worth, it is definitely going to be an educated guess at best.

Real estate agents usually base these subjective estimates on the selling price of other properties. For example, if you live in a subdivision, it may be easier to determine the value of your property because there are other similar homes to compare it to. In a subdivision, the models, floor plans, and age of the homes are similar. However, you should go even further and examine other subdivisions in surrounding areas to get a more complete picture. By scoping other potentially competing properties, you can get a clearer estimate of the current value of your home.

Pricing Your Property

Now that you have a better idea of how the value of a property is determined, let's look at how to compare property prices. When most home sellers are comparing the values of properties, they tend to look at the prices of properties that have already been sold. They then try to set their selling price off that information.

However, there is a different perspective that will serve you much better. I suggest that you look at *active* properties on the market as well as those that are under contract. Why would you spend time doing this? Well, if you focus on properties that have already been sold, you may fail to realize what is going on in the market at that particular time. As a result, you may end up under-pricing your home.

It is possible that there are currently no homes on the market for sale, which means demand is likely to be high. You should also look at any properties that were about to be sold but the deal was either canceled or expired. Find out why these properties weren't sold. Is it because they were overpriced, or was it an issue with the location? You may assume that a deal was canceled due to a high selling price and thus underprice your home, yet the real reason could be something else entirely.

The truth is that there are many bits of information that you have to consider and put together to determine what your home is worth. And even when you do, you'll still be making an educated guess because you can never have all the details. At the end of the day, the value of your property will simply be determined by the market itself.

Temper Your Optimism

From my experience, the vast majority of home sellers are extremely optimistic when it comes to valuing their properties; 90% of home sellers tend to think that their homes are worth more than they really are. This is usually a result of emotional attachment to the home, which means you will only focus on the good aspects of your property. If nobody steps up to tell you otherwise, you will stick to a price that is way higher than what the market can bear. It is only on rare occasions when a home seller undervalues their home or has no clue what the value of their home is. In such situations, the real estate agent should be able to help them make a price determination.

If there's one thing you should understand, it is this: There are many costs, factors, and conditions that play a role in the pricing of a piece of property. Ultimately, the only way of knowing the true worth of your home is by placing it on the market.

In the next chapter, you will learn some key strategies that will help you price your home properly.

♦ ♦ ♦

I would love to set up a complimentary consultation with you! Please reach out to me through my website at www.BrianErnst.net. Also, if you would like to be connected with a wonderful agent in your area, please visit www.BrianErnst.net.

Unsure about whether you need an agent or not? Reach out and I will personally connect you to an agent to simply have a discussion. You are still in control, and you get to decide what will work best for you!

Chapter Two

How to Price Your Home

Figuring out what price to set for your home is often a challenge to most home sellers. The pressure of setting the price too high and not selling or too low and losing money can upset anyone. The majority go too high, some underprice their homes, while a few have no idea whatsoever. Regardless of which category you are in, my advice is always to price your property as competitively as possible. You have to look at other homes that are also on sale and set a competitive price because buyers will always base their decisions on comparative pricing. If buyers believe that your home offers them the best value for their needs, they are more likely to buy from you.

Do you remember what you learned in Chapter 1 about home value?

The value of your home is subjective, which means it's based on many market variables, and all you can do is make an educated guess. However, there are particular elements that do increase the value of your home. For example, a spacious home will be priced higher than a smaller one. A home that offers greater privacy is likely to be more valuable than one that has less privacy. The features and functionality that your home offers will also determine its value. With the right strategies, you can attract buyers who will offer you the price you are looking for.

So, what are some of these pricing strategies that you can use?

Pricing Strategies

One of the most effective pricing strategies is to price your home as close to the market value as possible. You have already learned what kind of questions to ask and the factors to focus on. Armed with this information, it becomes easier to estimate your home's market value.

One thing I always discourage clients from is the tendency to set a price that leaves room for negotiation. This is a terrible strategy for one simple reason. Most sellers tend to overprice their homes anyway. They think that if they set a much higher price, they can still walk away with a tidy sum even if the buyer negotiates the price downward. The negotiating room seems like a good idea, but let me paint a different perspective with the following potential scenario.

Imagine you price your home as close to market value as possible and receive three competing offers. In this case, you can play the buyers against one another and end up receiving a full price or possibly even higher than your listing price. Now, imagine you overprice your home because you want to leave room for negotiation. You could end up with one offer, but because there are no other interested buyers competing for your home, you lose leverage, and the negotiation turns into a game. You make an offer, and the buyer makes their counteroffer. The buyer may say something like, "Hey, but I have to put in new flooring," expecting that this argument is enough for you to drop your price. But what do the buyer's personal tastes have to do with anything? As far as you're concerned, the flooring is absolutely fine. Besides, they may want to change the flooring in any home they buy.

Do you see my point here?

By pricing as close to market value as possible, you can end up with more offers and avoid such pointless arguments that usually arise when you have only one interested buyer. If you have three offers on the table, you don't have to pander to the tastes of one person who is raising irrelevant arguments. This changes the dynamics of the negotiation.

I'm not trying to say that the buyer's needs are illogical. Sure, they have their needs as well. My point is that there's no need for you to waste time when you can price your home on the money and sell it quicker. This will save you months of mortgage payments, insurance, taxes, utilities, and liability costs.

This is what you need to understand. It's better to have a bunch of offers all day long and turn them down rather than only having one offer. That one offer may be really low, and in some cases, the low-balling buyer may still complain that the price is too high. You don't want to put yourself in that position.

Sticking to Your Guns

As always, there are some sellers who choose to ignore my advice and decide to stick to their high prices. They argue that they aren't in a hurry to sell their homes, so they can afford to wait and see if buyers takes the bait.

In such cases, I wouldn't bother listing their home. It's simply a waste of time, money, and effort for the both of us. Why go through all that stress waiting for a buyer for your overpriced home? Do you think that buyers are ignorant and don't have access to the information that you do? Heck, in most cases, buyers are represented by their own agents who have done their own homework and understand the market conditions, so you will probably be wasting their time as well.

I've seen some sellers list their properties at exorbitant prices, and they end up spending years waiting for buyers. There have been cases where such situations have caused so much stress that people get divorced. So, sticking to your guns is simply a ridiculous strategy.

Have there been cases where an overpriced home gets sold? Yes, but there are also some homes that get sold for ridiculously low prices. These are rare cases, just like winning the lottery. Yet, people tend to hold onto such ideas, hoping that it's their turn to cash in big. The truth is that you don't know why that overpriced home was bought. Maybe the market conditions were right. The timing and location were right. Maybe the buyer needed to move quickly because their kids had to get into school by a certain time frame. The buyer could have paid in cash so there was no appraisal to stop the deal.

The bottom line is that these are unique and rare situations that you shouldn't rely on when pricing your home. Price it as close to market value as possible and save yourself the regrets. Learn to be flexible and adapt to changing situations. Sometimes the parties involved in a deal, rather than the market, are the ones that can change a situation. In the next chapter, you'll learn how home appraisals by third parties work.

Chapter Three

Understanding How Appraisals Work

If you plan on selling your home, then it's best that you understand a bit about appraisals and how they may affect the sale of your property.

An appraisal occurs when the buyer intends to apply for a loan from a bank to finance the purchase of a piece of property. Since the bank must protect its interests on the loan, it requests a neutral third party to determine the market value of the property the buyer is interested in acquiring. This third party is known as an appraisal management company.

Thanks to the current mortgage regulations that were introduced over a decade ago, the lender does not talk directly to the appraiser. These regulations are designed to protect the consumer, and since the appraiser is not tied to the deal in any way, they will be neutral in their thought process.

What does this mean for the home seller?

Well, the first thing you should understand is that you are not tied into the deal moving forward. Let's say that you have an agreed contract with the potential buyer and the appraisal process has begun. If the appraiser determines that your home is worth less than the contract price, it doesn't mean that you are obligated to sell for that lower value. You can still negotiate directly with the buyer and ask them to pay above the appraised value.

The challenge is that the loan the buyer is receiving from the lender is determined by the appraisal value. If the appraisal value is lower than the selling price, the bank will only give the buyer what the appraiser has determined to be the actual value of the property. Another issue is the percentage of down payment the buyer pays the bank. If the appraisal is below the sale price, then the down payment will be based on the appraised value, not the sale price of the home. However, if the appraisal is higher than the sale price, which is quite rare, then the loan down payment will be based on the sale price.

So, what options do you have at this point?

How to Handle a Lower Appraisal

In a case where the appraisal comes in lower than the price you agreed upon with the buyer, you have three options:

- **Option 1:** Agree to sell at the appraised price.

- **Option 2:** Insist that the buyer pays the price agreed upon in the contract. If the buyer is putting down 10% for the loan down payment and the appraisal is off by $10,000, they will have to cough up the selling price *plus* the loan down payment. Most buyers simply don't have that extra money. However, it is possible that the buyer has fallen in love with some of the unique features of your home that weren't factored into the appraised value. If so, then the buyer may be willing to pay your asking price. In my experience, I have seen appraisals that are almost irrelevant because the appraiser didn't consider the unique features of a property. Therefore, the appraised value was not correct. Fortunately, the buyer may see things differently and still want to find a way to purchase the home.

- **Option 3:** Refuse to sell the property. You are not obligated to accept the appraised value. If the buyer wants to move forward, it's up to them to find a way to make Option 2 work.

Years ago, after the market began to recover from the crash in 2008, appraisers were afraid of valuing a home too high because they didn't want the banks and appraisal management companies to blackball them. As a result, I have had years where many of my properties didn't appraise out. I remember one particular week where three appraisals went bad. However, in the last year alone, all my properties have been appraised out. That shows you how appraisals are affected by market conditions and changes in home values.

Other than appraisals, there are other factors to consider when selling a home. Another main part of this process is how much to pay your real estate agent. That's what you will learn in the next chapter.

Chapter Four

Agent Fees and Commissions

One of the most important factors to a home seller is the amount of money that they will have to pay their real estate agent. It's easy to fall into the trap of hiring an agent who charges less just to save money. But there's a lot that goes into the fees and/ or commissions that agents charge their clients. In fact, did you know that all commission gets paid directly to the agents' brokerage, which takes its cut before paying the agent?

If we look at the way relocation companies work in regard to commission, it may help you better understand how commissions are paid out. Relocation companies are found all over the United States. Most of the ones that I have worked with charge a 6% commission with the listing. This commission varies according to the location, price range, and services provided. For example, some areas are going to attract a higher commission than others, with the sale price of the home also affecting the commission amount.

It is very important to know that there is no standard commission that you are expected to pay an agent. This is true for most states in the United States. A portion of the commission goes to pay the buyer's agent fees, and the other portion goes to the listing agent. The agent's actual commission can be 10%, or it may even be a penny for all we know! Right now, we have states that have imposed or proposed laws to limit the commissions that real estate agents are paid.

Should Agent Commissions Be Your Priority?

If your main worry is how much money you will end up paying in agent commissions, then I must tell you that you are totally missing the point.

Why do I say this?

Because you are not asking the right question!

The question you need to be asking is, "How can this agent get me more money than anybody else?" Here's an example to help you understand the difference between these two perspectives. Let's say you have three agents. Agent Amy charges a 5% commission, Agent Barry charges 6%, and Agent Carlos charges 7%. If Agent Carlos is using more services, has access to greater resources, and is employing more effective marketing techniques to get your home sold at a higher price, who cares whether they are charging 2% more than Agent Amy?

Maybe the reason why the other two agents are cheaper is that they don't have the same capacity to get your home sold at that higher sale price. So, you may want to be cheap and skimp on the agent commissions, but you end up paying for it when your home doesn't sell at the price you wanted. Heck, you'll be lucky if they sell your home at all!

Another factor that should take precedence is the experience level of each agent. You want to be working with an agent who has more experience because they will be better able to solve your problems. When a crisis erupts, you don't want to get stuck with an inexperienced agent who charges you a lower commission. In fact, an inexperienced agent is more likely to make mistakes that will ultimately cost you more money. And that means you'll end up getting less money from the sale of your home. An inexperienced agent could also cost you a deal, which means you now have to make another mortgage payment, not to mention utilities, taxes, insurance, etc.

Are you still willing to focus on agent commissions over experience level?

Here's my advice to you. The amount of money you pay your agent should be commensurate to the value that they bring to the table. Once you understand the value of your agent, then their commission becomes a minor issue. From my experience, between 2% and 4% of the commision goes to paying the seller's agent. So, focus on the value they bring and how much money you will end up with at the end of the deal.

Paying the Agent's Fees

In most cases, the seller of the property is the one who pays the agent's commission. The only time the buyer pays the fees is when there is a buyer agency agreement. In the event that the seller of the property does not have an agent and is therefore selling the home "By Owner," then the seller usually won't pay out any commission to any agents. The agent representing the buyer then has to have a buyer agency agreement with the buyer so that the buyer pays them a commission in exchange for their services. This is a common clause that is found in a buyer's agreement in every state. However, in the majority of cases, it is the seller who ends up covering the agent fees.

When it comes to agent commissions, there are many factors to consider. Don't get caught up on higher versus lower percentage fees. You want to walk away with as much money as possible and as quickly as possible. The right agent can help you do that. In the next chapter, we'll talk about how long it should take to sell your home.

◆　◆　◆

If you would like to schedule a complimentary consultation, please visit my website at www.BrianErnst.net.

Chapter Five

How Fast Can You Sell My Home?

Every home seller wants to know the answer to this question. In general, there are three factors that determine how long it takes to sell a home. These are the location of the property, its condition, and pricing.

Location

Out of all the factors, this is the one that you have the least control over. You can't just pick up your home and move it somewhere else where the demand is higher. The location of your home is already fixed, so you simply have to deal with that. When we talk about location, you should also examine the environment around your home and how it affects the value of your property.

For example, what kind of neighborhood do you live in? Is it clean or run-down? What structures are being built in the area that might affect the value of your home? A garbage dump being built close to your home will definitely impact the value of your property and how long it takes to sell.

Condition

As a home seller, you can actually do something about the condition of your home to help get it sold faster. But there is a catch. How much money are you willing to spend to improve the condition of your home to attract buyers? How much time and effort are you willing to put in for a faster and potentially higher sales price?

You may decide to turn it into a DIY project, but even then, you'll still have to buy supplies, materials, and equipment to update the property. You have to ask yourself whether it's really worth it. My recommendation is that you get your home into the best possible condition you can manage. The better the condition of your home, the faster it is likely to sell, assuming that you price it accordingly.

Pricing

If you price your home according to market value, it will sell fairly quickly. But this price will also depend on the other two factors already mentioned. The market value of your property is dependent on its condition and location. As you can see, it's the intricate interplay among these three factors that determine how fast the home sells within the current market conditions.

Most homes tend to sell within the first week or two if priced correctly. You don't need to have many people looking at your property to purchase it. All you need is one potential buyer to love your home before somebody buys it. I usually tell my sellers that for every person who views your property, they will, on average, look at 10 other homes. Therefore, if you have 10 showings within two weeks and the potential buyers compared your property to 10 others, that means there are a total of 100 comparisons. If you don't get an acceptable offer out of these 100 comparisons, then it's likely that your property is not priced correctly according to its condition and location. Your home is essentially overpriced for that current market.

Keep in mind that the homes that I'm referring to are the type that the average person lives in. I'm not referring to some $6 million home on a ranch in the middle of nowhere. This is a totally different market. When I talk about the length of time it takes to sell a home, I'm talking about a home that is in a location where you have easy access to the train or bus so that people can get to work or school. I'm talking about a home that is located in a place where you can get between 5 to 20 showings over a span of 30 days.

In general, the lower your price range, the more the number of showings a home gets. That also means the greater the number of people who can afford it. If the price is high, fewer buyers can afford it, which circles back to fewer showings. A home with a high price range generally attracts a specific demographic that may be interested in its unique features. For example, if your home has features such as a gold-plated toilet seat or an Olympic-sized pool, then the high price range will obviously keep away regular buyers.

So, if you want to know how long it is going to take to sell your home, consider its location, condition, and price range. There's not much you can do about location, but there are definitely steps you can take to make your home more attractive to buyers. We'll learn more about this in the next chapter.

Chapter Six

Staging Your Home

How important is it to stage your home to sell it? Should you put in the time and effort or leave it as is? There is no straightforward answer to these questions because it all depends on the type of property you are trying to sell. There are times when it would be a good idea to stage your home, and sometimes, it wouldn't really help at all.

There are instances in which I have sold properties where it was best not to stage the home. Instead, we simply focused on preparing the home for sale. In fact, there are times when staging the home can be detrimental to the sale of the home. If your home is small and you decide to stuff all kinds of fancy furniture in there just to impress a buyer, it's going to work against you. Of course, there are times when staging does a great deal to make the home look better. Adding some nice furniture and decorations can sometimes help sell the home much faster.

Many types of properties can move very quickly without any staging. In such types of homes, there would be very little value added by spending time and money staging the property.

From my experience, homes that have a higher price range tend to require more staging because people will want to know why the price is so high. For such homes, you want to show off the style as well as the functionality. High-end buyers are always looking out for more than just your average, functional home. They are paying for the extra features.

Think of it like a car. There are expensive cars out there that have four doors, four wheels, and can move you from point A to B. But there are also much cheaper cars that look the same and serve the same function. Why are some priced higher than others? It's all about the features. Are the additional features in a luxury car proportionate to its value? From my experience, I don't think so. I am aware that there are people who are willing to spend money on the extra features when buying a car and a home. And in my opinion, that equates to value.

Hiring Professional Staging Services

If you decide to stage your home, then you should understand the cost and time factor involved. If you can't do it yourself, there are other options at your disposal. There are staging companies that can come in and get the job done within a week. You will have to rent their pieces of furniture and decorations for a given period of time. You should know that not all staging companies are the same. You have to do your research and get recommendations from experienced professionals.

There are also real estate agents who offer staging recommendations and coaching as part of their services. When my clients ask me whether I have a stager, I offer them my services because this is something I have been doing for over 16 years. You won't have to bring in any new furniture or decorations. I know how to simply work with what you already have.

For those who have don't have the kind of furniture that we can use for staging, I recommend that they remove any items that are mismatched, in poor condition, or don't fit in the room. If you have two couches, two chairs, a coffee table, and a TV in one room, leaving only one couch can create more space and make the room look much bigger. The perception of extra space can make your home feel like it has more square footage. This is why I always recommend that people take more furniture out rather than keeping a room stuffed full of furniture. Sometimes, staging a home is as simple as taking one piece out.

Whether you decide to do it yourself or hire a professional company, the most important thing that I can tell you about staging is this: If the condition of your home is not good, then staging can only take you so far. I would rather you focus on upgrading the condition of your home and preparing it for sale. In the next chapter, I will explain some strategies for this.

Chapter Seven

Preparing Your Home for Sale

There is a lot that you can do to make sure that your home is ready for sale. Apart from particular strategies that you can use, you should be prepared to adjust your mindset and also work with an experienced agent who can guide you along the process.

Before we get into that, there's one tip that I always share. As a seller, the best thing you can do to prepare your home is to ensure that it is in the best condition possible from day one of a listing. You should begin preparing your home for buyers so that the day that you list your home for sale, it is as good as you can make it. It's no use changing its condition after it has been on the market for a period of time and some buyers have already viewed it, not been impressed, and moved on.

Why do I say this?

Because the buyers who will visit your home at the beginning of a listing are the ones who are ready and able to close a deal. Those who come, say, two to three weeks later are usually new buyers who have just entered the market. They are merely browsing around and do not have the same urgency as the earlier ones. You lost the first ones because they will have already purchased their new home. They are lost to you.

Now, let's talk about what you can do to prepare your property for sale so you don't lose a qualified buyer.

Strategies for Preparing Your Home for Sale

Some of the factors you need to consider when preparing your home include painting, flooring, updating certain appliances and light fixtures, etc. Apart from working on the interior, there are also external adjustments you can make to improve your property's curb appeal. Landscaping is a great example of this. Basic or even deep cleaning may be a necessary step for both interior and exterior.

Think of it like buying a used car. When you go to purchase a used vehicle, you expect to see a car that is washed, waxed, and perfectly clean. The interior should also be spotless. However, most people rarely look under the hood at the mechanics of the vehicle. And that's the same with home buyers. They won't focus on the mechanicals of the property. So, I always recommend to my clients that they focus on the most obvious issues that need to be repaired, especially the cosmetic stuff.

Usually around 90% of my clients need to paint their homes, install new flooring, replace the carpeting, clean the windows, replace broken window seals, and make other cosmetic repairs. If we start talking about the mechanicals of the property and how they are out of code for that specific area, then that's a whole different conversation. We talk about all this when dealing with the pricing of your home. So, for the purpose of preparing your home for sale, we usually stick to the cosmetic repairs.

How Home Preparation Affects the Sale

Preparing your home for sale all comes down to doing whatever will provide the best return on your investments. For example, most people cannot see through paint colors. A good coat of paint can easily cover up some defect on your wall, and the buyer will hardly notice it. If this is the case and you snag multiple offers, then clearly, giving your home a good paint job is a great return on that investment.

However, if the buyer does see a defect and still chooses to buy your home, they will try to calculate what they think it would cost to repair it. Unfortunately, buyers usually triple the cost of the repairs because most of them are not contractors. They don't have the relevant experience when it comes to upgrading a property, and they also factor in the time it would take. In their minds, the cost of repairs becomes more significant than it actually is in reality. As a result, they will want the seller to lower the price of the property, even if the seller has already priced their home according to proper market value for its condition.

This is why it's important to make sure that your home is updated and ready for sale. You need to make your home desirable so that you can be in a multiple-offer situation. Even if you price it correctly for a non-outdated property, without the necessary cosmetic preparations, you won't get the best price possible. The buyer's offer will be significantly lower than what you expect to receive.

Here's what I mean.

Let's say it costs you about $10,000 to paint your home, redo the flooring, and perform some minor repairs. Since most buyers won't be able to see through the cosmetic upgrades, the difference in sale price could be as much as $30,000. But if a buyer walks in and says things like, "I don't like this. It needs to be repainted, and this part is dirty," then they won't be motivated to pay full price. Ultimately, the best homes with the highest resale values are properties that are ready to be moved into. The buyer doesn't have to fix anything. This is true for all kinds of properties, from inexpensive ones all the way to the high-end ones.

If you make the right preparations, then the difference in cost can be significant. On the flip side, you don't want to go as far as making major repairs such as replacing interior doors, hinges, handles, and similar things. This is a slippery slope that won't give you the best return on investment because you'll be wasting market time engaging in too many repairs.

Get Your Mindset Right

There are some home sellers who have a hard time understanding the importance of making basic upgrades to their home for sale. They argue that it's okay to let the buyer replace the paint, flooring, and carpeting according to their own preferences. The buyer may have their own preferences, so why waste time and money doing the repairs for them, right?

While this argument may make some sense, it is definitely the wrong mindset to have as a seller. Here's the deal. Very few buyers are looking to remodel a home. The small percentage who are willing to do so are usually people who are looking to get some kind of a discount. So, you are essentially limiting yourself to a small demographic of buyers. The majority of buyers do not have that extra 10, 20, or 30 grand to remodel a home since they have a down payment to make as well. They have to get to work, take their children to school, and move on with their lives. The average buyer has no time or money to become a pseudo-contractor, running around repairing and remodeling the property.

This is what I tell my clients all the time. Invest the money on repairs now so that you don't get a significantly lower price offer. This lazy attitude is quite common because sellers want to take the easy way out. Why would you want to do something that will limit your pool of buyers? Just put in a little work ahead of time to avoid pain in the long run. If you're lazy and decide to pass the work off to your buyer, then the joke is on you.

If you don't want to do it and the buyer doesn't want to do it, then your home will not sell!

Of course, there is still the possibility that you will sell the home without doing any repairs whatsoever. But there is such a small chance for that outcome compared the likelihood of selling your home when you've taken action that is likely to appeal to the broadest possible audience. You want to have many offers on the table so that you have choices. Otherwise, you may end up with very few offers, or in some cases, one bad offer. And you'll be lucky if that cheapskate buyer ever follows through with the whole deal.

Working with an Agent When Preparing Your Home

It's always a good idea to work with an experienced real estate agent when preparing your property for sale. There are some aspects of home preparation that are not as straightforward as you may think. Sometimes, having someone with the required knowledge can be the difference between making a sale and getting stuck with a home that you've spent money on repairing.

Let's say you have a home that is 20 years old. It has all the same fittings, fixtures, and appliances that were in common use two decades ago. If you were selling the home, would you update the paint and carpet and leave all the original brass fittings and fixtures in place? Or would you also replace the faucets, counters, and those types of things?

In such a situation, there is no easy answer. It would depend on what the market is bearing in your particular area. In some areas, you may get away with doing nothing because the demand for homes is so high. If you are in a true seller's market, you can get away with more compared to when you are in a buyer's market. In most cases, the correct answer is somewhere in between.

You already know that it's always a good idea to have a home that is move-in ready. However, if you take care of the flooring and painting and the other properties around you have been updated better, then you'll still lose out. This is where a qualified agent comes in handy. Having an experienced and capable real estate agent will save you a lot of hassle and money. The agent can walk through the other open homes in the area and gauge how move-in ready they are compared to yours. They can look at the fixtures of other properties and let you know what you are competing against.

Your ability to walk through other open homes to gauge the market for yourself is limited. You will probably only get to view a handful of properties. But a qualified agent can do this for you and give you the advice you need to prepare your home for sale in the best way possible. Reading a bunch of books on home preparation may not necessarily help either. The books may advise you to replace the kitchen counters, but if the majority of the other homes in the area have not updated their kitchen counters, then there's no need to spend money on that. It won't have a direct impact on your sale price.

An experienced agent will be able to tell you what to spend money on and what to ignore. If everyone else is replacing their appliances, they will advise you to do the same. This kind of advice is what can be a make or break a decision when it comes to selling your home.

Preparing your home can involve basic cleaning or more extensive repairs. You should be mentally prepared to work with an experienced agent who will ensure you get the best return on your investment. Of course, you cannot sell your home if nobody knows that it is for sale in the first place. So, in the next chapter, I'll show you how the listing and advertising process works.

◆　◆　◆

If you would like to schedule a complimentary consultation, please visit my website at www.BrianErnst.net.

Chapter Eight

Listing and Advertising Your Home

Part of the process of selling your home is getting it listed and advertised. This is how your property will get exposed to potential buyers who are searching for a home that fits a certain criteria. Therefore, it is important for every seller to understand how real estate listing and advertising works.

Multiple Listing Services (MLS)

When you are selling your home, it has to be listed on the multiple listing services. A licensed real estate agent who is part of a board (and therefore also a part of the National Association of Realtors) is allowed to list your home on the MLS. It's important to note that not all licensed agents are part of this board. Those agents who are not part of the MLS find it very difficult to list and sell homes. Only those who have this higher-level designation are able to list your property so that every other licensed agent with access can see it. This is the case all across the country, though there are some differences in certain areas.

Another thing you should know is that just because an agent has access to and can list your property on the MLS doesn't mean they are going to do it well. The agent has to do it the right way so that the information can filter out to other relevant websites. Years ago, the information on the MLS could only be accessed within the platform. The only people who could see it were the agents who had access to the MLS.

However, things have changed now. Today, there are many different websites that pull information from the MLS and have feeds that are publicly accessible. For example, Trulia, Zillow, and realtor.com all have access to the MLS and provide this information on their websites. So, the agent who you are working with has to meet the requirements and set it up right, otherwise nobody will see your listing outside the MLS.

Maximizing the Use of the MLS

What does a realtor have to do to ensure that they list your home properly in the MLS?

To maximize the use of the MLS, the agent needs to fill out all the important criteria in the MLS. This is quite an extensive process. For example, there are some people who search for a subdivision by name. An agent who does not know this information may choose not to fill it out because it is not a requirement in the MLS. However, if another agent is looking for homes in that specific subdivision, the listed home will not show up in the search results. The MLS will not show that home because the agent who listed it didn't add the information, and the agent who is searching doesn't know how to dig deeper to find it.

The agent who is searching for a home in the subdivision can do a map search or a rubber band search where you loop around whatever area you want. They can also select specific streets. But if they just use the name of the subdivision, that information won't be pulled up because it's not a required field. Let's say the listing agent fills in the school district but not the name of a high school. Another agent who is searching the MLS for that specific high school won't find the information. These are the kinds of issues that happen when an agent doesn't know how to maximize the use of the MLS.

Another factor to note is the description of the property. The agent has to ensure that they've described the home well, especially the features that can't be seen in pictures. The photos should be of high quality, but not too good that the buyer can see all the flaws in a property. There are times when the highest-quality photos are not the best asset for a particular property.

As a real estate agent, it is my job to list the property the right way and get people into the property. So, if the home isn't listed properly on the MLS, its exposure to potential buyers will be limited.

Marketing Techniques

Apart from the listing, there's also the marketing aspect to think about. The act of placing your home on the MLS doesn't mean it will get enough exposure to make a sale. The success of your marketing will depend on the agent you are working with and the types of marketing techniques they have at their disposal. These include:

1. **Websites.** When I list a home on the MLS, I do everything to make sure that there's maximum exposure. I work with a variety of websites and employ different marketing strategies to ensure that my listings are seen by as many people as possible. The goal is to make sure that people can see my listings on tens of thousands of different websites through the MLS. Once they see it, they will come looking for more information. I'm very careful about the kind of websites I work

with because some of them are just full of misinformation. We don't want to deceive the public.

2. **Direct marketing.** I also do a lot of direct marketing and mailings to specific people within the same geographical area. If there are people who want to move up or down in size, they can see what I have available on my listings. I also use certain websites where I arrange the listings differently than the ones that rely on automatic feeds from the MLS.

3. **Open houses.** Another extensive marketing technique is open houses. Most people think that it's the *open house* that's the thing. No, it's all about the marketing *behind* the open house. For example, I'll advertise on social media about a "coming-soon" property that is not even on the market yet, and the only people who have access are the agents. This builds up a ton of interest before the home is even ready to be shown. We target people who we believe would be the most interested in coming to see us.

4. **Videos.** We also take videos of the property to attract potential buyers. Videos are a great way to let people have a feel of the home. But we don't give them a feel to get them to come in the door. The aim is to make sure that the homes they see fit their criteria. Since homes sell homes, potential buyers will compare the homes they see on video, and this will generate even greater interest. Of course, when we create these videos, we don't show people everything. If we did, people would make their decision there and then, and some would lose interest. We only put out enough information for marketing purposes. I provide more details about this in Chapter 19.

5. **Hiring other companies.** I also use other companies as a marketing tool to expose my properties in different places. Most of these companies use the internet to market my properties. About 15 years ago, we would probably advertise in the local newspaper and take out magazine ads. Today, 99% of people are searching for properties on the internet.

As you can see, you need to work with a savvy and experienced agent who will be able to list your home and maximize the use of the MLS. On top of that, the agent has to have strong marketing tools at their disposal to get buyers through your door. Some marketing techniques are more effective than others depending on the situation. In the same way, when it comes to the real estate world, not all agents are created equal. With that said, let's talk about some of the expectations you need to have of a real estate agent.

Chapter Nine

Roles and Responsibilities of a Real Estate Agent

As a home seller, there are certain tasks that you expect a real estate agent to do. It is important to understand the roles and responsibilities of your listing agent so that you don't waste your time with an agent who doesn't have a clue what they are supposed to do. Your agent should be able to work through any kind of unforeseen issues that may arise, whether it's through their own experience or by leveraging their network.

So, what are some of the functions of a listing agent?

There are three major areas of responsibility:

1. **Listing and marketing.** Your agent should list your home and market your property to the public to get as many people through the door as possible. The agent should be promoting the home to qualified buyers who fit the criteria to see the property.

2. **Advisory role.** It is your agent's job to act as your advisor when it comes to preparing the home for sale and dealing with all the transactions.

3. **Representing your interests.** Your agent should always be working to protect your interests throughout the process of selling your home.

The national statistics on real estate agents paint a grim picture, and they show that most agents do not do the most brilliant job. And that's where experience and skill comes in. I have been in the industry long enough to know how to get my clients the most money in the least amount of time. I understand what my responsibilities are, and as a result, I set the proper expectations to maximize what my clients put in their pockets at the end of the day.

Hiring the Right Agent for the Job

For some strange reason, quite a number of home sellers think that they can act as their own real estate agents. They think that they can easily fit into the role and get the job done. It is this kind of assumption that can get you into huge trouble.

Why do I say this?

I have closed well over a thousand real estate deals, and even I can't predict how every step of the process will play out. It's simply not possible because you are dealing with human beings, and every situation is entirely different. You can't describe what the process is going to entail because it's dependent on who you are dealing with, bank schedules, and how many other issues come up. Every deal is different, and the parties in the deal also change over time. So, even if you are dealing with the same group of people but at a different time, the situation won't be the same as before.

If I, with all my decades of experience, can attest to this, what do you think is going to happen when a seller with no experience decides to become his or her own agent?

Things are likely to go sideways very quickly when sellers think they can do it on their own or hire an inexperienced agent who charges a lower commision. This is not the kind of job that just anybody can do. I can't tell you how many stories I have about home sellers being given bad advice that ends up costing them a small fortune. We're talking $10,000 mistakes here and there, simply because a seller listened to the wrong agent who told them to do the wrong things, or even the right things in the wrong order.

Part of an agent's job is to recommend to you the right lenders, attorneys, and home inspectors. If you are working with someone who doesn't know what they are doing, you could be led down a path that leads to a canceled deal. This also applies when you, the seller, are also looking to buy a home. You shouldn't just use anybody to help you buy a home.

I had a case where a seller came to me to list their home because they knew my track record and experience when it comes to selling property. However, they decided to work with someone else when it came to buying a new home. Unfortunately, they didn't realize that the real estate agent they were using had recommended a lender that they didn't have enough experience with. The lender gave the buyer the impression that everything was fine and the deal could proceed. Fast forward 30 days later, and I had their property on the market. I was receiving offer after offer, and we even had it under contract at this point. All of a sudden, the lender said, "No, I can't do the deal." If they had come to me, I would have recommended a lender that would have figured the financial problem out within the first 24 hours of working with them. Because of this mistake, they lost precious time as well as $10,000.

Luckily, they learned their lesson pretty quickly. They came to me, and I recommended a lender who I've fully vetted as I have done hundreds of deals with them. We were able to get them a less expensive and much bigger home in the same area, and I was also able to sell their home very quickly again. They managed to do better than they thought they would, but it was still a $10,000 lesson.

These kinds of mistakes happen a lot. With all my experience, I can't explain to you what could possibly come up during every deal. This is something that you figure out when you get into it. This is why I say that you need to work with an agent who has enough experience to get you through the deal. The agent doesn't really control anything. They are busy facilitating communications between all the parties involved. A lot of things can happen from the moment a home is listed until it goes under contract. But it's never over until the deal closes.

The Art of the Deal

I cannot stress enough the importance of working with people who have massive experience in their fields. It will save you a lot of time, money, energy, and grief.

I recently had a client who wanted to sell their home. Usually, I ask my clients a whole list of questions to make sure that I know everything that's going on before I even list their properties. For some reason, this client didn't bring up the fact that they had a judgment against them. We only found out about it when their home was under contract. The judgment was for $600,000, yet the home they were selling was priced at less than $300,000.

In some cases, a judgment can be a lien on a home. If a contractor doesn't get paid for something, they can put a lien on your home to ensure that if it ever gets sold, they get paid what they are owed. A lien on a home might have been placed recently or even 10 years ago. In this case, we had a court order that said that my client had to pay $600,000 in restitutions for some previous contract breach. This means that the person they owed money to would take every cent they would make from the proceeds of this home sale.

Even with experience, I had no idea how to handle this situation. There's no way my client would sell his home just to walk away with nothing. Because I work with experienced people, I involved my attorney, who managed to negotiate a deal with the bank that had the judgment against my client. My attorney told the bank, "Look, just let him sell his home and allow him to walk away with $20,000 of the equity. You can take the rest of the money and slap a judgment on him for his next property. But if you stick to your guns and do it the way you're doing it right now, he won't sell, and you will get nothing. Would you rather get paid something and have another property to attach to, or would you rather have nothing?"

What do you think the bank did?

Now, I didn't think of this strategy right away. But because I work with such experienced people, I am able to get through this kind of problematic deal. The attorney I work with on the majority of deals does more than 2,000 deals a year, so he understands how different real estate transactions are handled.

An agent cannot know or see everything, no matter how many transactions they have closed. This is why we need people around us who know their stuff. And the guys I roll with know their stuff. One thing I definitely do know is how to sell homes quickly. So, in the next chapter, we'll dive into that.

◆　◆　◆

If you would like to schedule a complimentary consultation, please visit my website at www.BrianErnst.net.

Chapter Ten

How to Sell Your Home as Fast as Possible

There are a number of factors that determine how long it takes to sell your home. The two major factors are the price of the home and its condition relative to the market.

The Price Factor

A listing price is subjective to your specific property, which means it's based off of other relevant or comparable properties. What other similar properties have been sold over the last three, six, or even 12 months? We also look at other homes that are active on the market, what's under contract right now, what has sold, and what hasn't sold. We use all this information to figure out what's a ballpark figure for the likely sale price of your home. This is not an exact science because the properties that have sold in the past are gone. The buyers who bought them are not in the market right now trying to buy another property unless they are investors.

Personally, I usually sell the majority of my properties within seven days. This is because my pricing strategy involves getting as close to the market value as possible. This way, my properties get the most exposure possible.

Most sellers believe in the notion that they should set a high price on their homes so as to leave room for negotiations with buyers. However, if you leave room for negotiations, you are leaving too much room for people to walk away without even putting an offer on the table. The buyers may think that the price is too high for them to afford, so they don't bid at all. They won't know that the seller has intentionally left some negotiating room.

An important fact that few people know about is that I cannot legally disclose to a buyer that there is room for negotiation. It's against real estate license law for me to do that without written permission from my sellers. So, if I advertise the price of a listed property, I cannot tell buyers that the seller is willing to drop the price by, say, $20,000. Therefore, I always advise my clients to price their homes at market value.

Lowering the price range of a property can make a massive difference, not just in terms of viewership but also in the number of people who are able to purchase it. You could have 10 times the viewership in the lower price range because the number of people who can afford the property increases as you lower the price. There are fewer people who can afford a million-dollar property versus a $50,000 property. The number of potential buyers increases exponentially as the price range goes down. Instead of merely doubling, sometimes the number of people who can purchase the property goes up 10 times.

The Condition Factor

Throughout my career, there have been very few instances where fixing up a property was irrelevant. In those years, the market was so hot for sellers that they didn't have to really do much to set up their homes. But for the majority of my career, those properties that have received upgrades are the ones that sell the fastest.

If a property is move-in ready, meaning it has been painted, the flooring looks good, and the appliances are all working properly, then it will attract more buyers. It is also important to update and style your home, because if it's too out of date, some buyers may lose interest. They may feel that they will have to rip out cabinets and undertake all kinds of major costly updates. From my experience, most buyers have already budgeted for their money and down payment, and they don't have any spare cash for upgrades and repairs. So, if your home is not in good condition, it will limit the number of people who can actually buy.

Out of every 10 buyers who come to view your property, how many do you think have and are willing to spend extra cash for renovation purposes? It is rare to hear a buyer say something like, "We'll get credit to fix this home. We'll see what they say and negotiate that out." No. Most buyers would simply walk away.

The length of time it takes to sell your home will depend on the price and condition of the property. Still, any kind of time frame I provide will be a guess at best because I cannot predict the future. I may be able to rely on past and present information, but that would still be inaccurate because market conditions can change literally hourly. The best thing to do is to call me and set up an appointment, and I'll come over to check out your home. We'll then determine what needs to be done and how to set it up. At that point, I may be able to provide a better estimate of the time frame.

Of course, if you are selling your home, you'll have to find somewhere else to live. So, in the next chapter, we'll talk about making other living arrangements and how to go about that.

Chapter Eleven

Finding a New Home Before Selling

Once you decide to put up your home for sale, you may feel the urge to find a new home before you actually sell your existing one. Is it always a good idea to find a home to buy first before selling the one you are currently living in?

There is no clear cut answer to this question because different people are in different situations. I would recommend that you have a general idea of where you want to move to and the kind of home you want. You don't have to find something with the *exact* tone and features that you have your heart set on. You can go ahead and find a home that fits your criteria in the neighborhood you want to move to. This is the most important thing.

I don't think it would be wise to actually find and buy a property before your existing home is sold. This is because 99% of people would not be able to afford it. The majority of people need to sell their home first before they buy another one because the purchase of the next home will typically be contingent on the sale of the original property. In other words, you need the proceeds from the sale of your existing home to buy a new one. And depending on your financial situation, most people simply don't qualify to carry two loans. You have to clear one loan to purchase the next one.

I would only recommend this option to the small percentage of people who already have the cash for buying the next place or have access to two loans and can make the payments. If you can afford to make double payments on BOTH your current and your new home, then go for it. You can move into a new home and not worry about how long it takes to sell your old property.

Understanding Home Sale Contingencies

If you decide to buy a home before you sell your current one, then the purchase contract on the property that you picked out is going to be a home sale contingency. This means that your ability to buy a new home is dependent on how fast you can sell your existing one. Since the seller that you made your offer to is taking a higher risk on you, they are likely to want more money from you. They will sell you the home at a much higher price to offset the risk of the deal collapsing. They are also limiting the exposure of their home to the market as long as your home remains unsold. Though they can still show it to other buyers, most agents choose not to. And this limits the viewership of their home on a map.

If I'm representing a seller and a buyer who hasn't sold their home yet comes in, I will advise my client to not accept their offer until the potential buyers have accepted a contract on their property. This is still highly risky because you have to wait for their deal to close for your own deal to close.

There's also the time factor to consider. If the seller accepts your offer with a home sale contingency, you are now forced to go and sell your home within a given time frame. The seller may give you 24-72 hours to get rid of your contingency. If you fail to close your end of the deal, you may end up with contractual issues. This can turn into a messy legal affair.

If you have to sell your current home as quickly as possible, do you think you are likely to sell it for more money or less? Since there's a time frame to consider, most people typically sell their homes for a lot less than would have otherwise been possible. This can happen all the while not even realizing that throughout the process, the property you think you have a contract on is not really yours yet. The seller can decide to kick you out if they find another buyer who doesn't have a home sale contingency.

At the end of it all, you are likely to end up paying more money for your new property and earning less from the sale of your current one. So, I always advise my clients that if they want to find a new property first, they should only have a general idea of the area they want to move to. They need to make sure that homes in that area are at least within the ballpark of reality of the prevailing market value and fall within their budget. Don't think that you are going to live in an area where the homes have four bedrooms, two and a half baths, finished basements, and are 3,000 square feet all for $200,000. Homes could be going for around $700,000 in that area you want. So, be realistic and sell your home first.

One thing that you should also be aware of is what is known as a reverse contingency. If you are putting your home on the market and are afraid that you won't find the home that you like, you can use this option. A reverse contingency is where you tell a prospective buyer that they can buy your home contingent upon you finding another property within a certain time period. This option is not widely used, and most buyers do not want to hear this from a seller. But if they are desperate for your property, they may accept your reverse contingency and give you some time to search for a home. All you have to do is give the buyer notice and keep them informed.

Alternative Options for Sellers

The majority of home sellers consider finding the home they want to buy first because they want to make sure that they have enough time to move out and into the new home. They don't want to move twice; that is, into a rental while they are waiting to sell their existing home and then into their new home.

Sellers need to know that they have alternative options beyond these ones. You can actually lease your home back from the new buyer. This is known as a *rent-back*. If you haven't found a home yet, you can request a rent-back option with the buyer while negotiating the sale contract. You essentially agree to rent the property from the buyer, who will be the new owner, for a set period of time. But you have to ask for this ahead of time, not when you're already in a contract.

In a rent-back situation, the buyer will hold back some of your proceeds as a deposit, and you agree to pay them rent for the number of days or months you'll be living in the home. Of course, the rent will be above market rate because the buyer doesn't want the situation to continue forever. They want to move into their new property as soon as possible. Though the terms may not be the fairest, at least you won't have to move twice.

Another option is locking in a mortgage at the start of the process. Most of my clients never have to move twice because they set everything up early on. If they need a mortgage, I set them up with the lenders that I usually work with, and everything gets done very quickly. On average, it takes 45 days to get a mortgage approved. I have lenders that can wrap everything up within two weeks, as long as you submit all your paperwork ahead of time and it goes through all the underwriting and review processes. It you think about it, you actually have about a whole month to find a property once you get yours under a contract and sort everything out with the lender. Then, all you have to do is pick out a property and close the deal in two weeks.

As long as you have the right people advising you and follow the right order, you won't face a lot of pressure. It definitely beats having to think about or do everything yourself. There are some tasks that you should simply leave to your agent because they have the necessary experience. In fact, in the next chapter, you will learn why it's a bad idea for you to personally market your own home.

◆　◆　◆

I would love to set up a complimentary consultation with you! Please reach out to me through my website at www.BrianErnst. net. Also, if you would like to be connected with a wonderful agent or lender in your area, please visit www.BrianErnst.net.

Unsure about whether you need an agent or lender? Reach out, and I will personally connect you with one to simply have a discussion. You are still in control, and you get to decide what will work best for you!

Chapter Twelve

Should I Market My Own Home?

The average home seller often assumes that they can personally market their own property. You may feel that you should at least help spread the word and offer some information about your home to as many potential buyers as possible. Seems like a good idea, right?

No, it isn't!

I wouldn't recommend that you engage in any kind of marketing of your own home. That is what you are paying your agent for. In fact, marketing your home can probably get you into situations that you don't want to be in. Once you start advertising your own property, all kinds of people will directly reach out to you for information, not knowing that you are represented by an agent. Even agents may reach out to you, and before you know it, you have unwittingly stuck your foot in your mouth while talking to a licensed agent.

I cannot tell you how many times I have had a seller say something potentially costly to an agent or a potential buyer during a negotiation. The buyer may ask a question, and since the seller is trying to be nice, they blab about something they shouldn't. Sometimes, this happens during a home inspection or the final walkthrough.

This speaks to the three major reasons why I never want my clients to meet the buyers until after the deal is closed:

1. **False claims from the buyer.** Sometimes, the buyer can claim that the seller of the property discriminated against them. But if the seller and the buyer never met, then this allegation falls flat on its face.

2. **Room for renegotiation.** When the seller is present during the closing, the buyer or their agent may try to renegotiate directly with them. By just being in the room, the seller creates the environment for renegotiation.

3. **Waste of time and money.** This usually comes up a lot during the final walkthrough and at the closings. There are times when I have asked a seller not to be present during a home inspection and they still show up. The seller then decides to explain some defects in the home to a licensed home inspector. The home inspector says, "Oh, that's not how that should be." Before you know it, the home inspector has documented it, and that ends up costing my client a lot of time and money. Something similar can also happen at the closing table or during the final walkthrough. Senario: We're sitting there with the seller, and the buyer asks for the garage door openers. The seller says, "Oh my gosh, we packed them up. They're already in Florida. We'll send them to you when we get there." All of a sudden, the buyer wants to hold $500 in escrow for garage door openers that cost 25 bucks! It's ridiculous the number of times something like this happens just because the home seller is present at the closing table. Sure, they are trying to be nice, but they can end up costing themselves money and wasting time.

Ultimately, it comes down to the issue of trust. Do you trust your agent to represent you in the best possible way? Some sellers want to be present in the meetings because they don't trust anybody. They refuse to rely on and trust in the professionals they have hired, and they start getting into conversations that they shouldn't be in. This can end up costing them a lot.

What You CAN Do to Market Your Home

If you really want to help market your home, then you can take your agent's advertisements and put them out there in your local area. Share them on social media, and make sure all the contact information leads directly to the agent and not yourself. If a potential buyer knocks on your door to ask for information, just tell them to call your agent. Show them the sign in the front yard with your agent's information, and tell them to call. Don't do or say anything else.

I have had clients who actually allowed potential buyers to enter their homes and take a look around. DON'T DO THIS, as there are safety concerns that can come up. I actually don't even want my clients to advertise their homes because it opens the door for people to have direct conversations with them. It may sound like a friendly conversation, but it may end up being an expensive one. You shouldn't have direct conversations with potential buyers, even if they are friends or family members who may live in the area. (Most of these advertisements are targeted at other people who don't live in the area, anyway.)

The best way to look at it is to see your real estate agent as you would an attorney. When you get arrested, you don't answer any questions until you've spoken with your attorney because the people interviewing you don't have your best interest in mind. The buyer and buyer's agent do not have your best interest in mind. Your agent does. Let them leverage their skills, abilities, and experience to protect your interests.

As you can see, there are times when a home seller should simply allow their agent to do what they are being paid to do. Blurring the lines can be costly and time-consuming.

◆　◆　◆

If you would like to schedule a complimentary consultation, please visit my website at www.BrianErnst.net.

Chapter Thirteen

Timing the Sale of Your Home

Is there a particular time that is best for selling your home? Home sellers tend to think that certain seasons or economic periods are best for selling. If there is such a thing as the perfect time, then it would make sense to wait for it so that you get the best price, possibly when demand is at its highest. However, I tell my sellers that the best time to sell a home is when you need to sell your home. If you are thinking of selling now, then now is the best time.

My reasoning is simple. I know what now is, but I don't know what things are going to look like six months from now. I'm a real estate agent, not a prophet. So, if you've already decided to move, do it now. We have no idea what factors and variables will come into play in the future. You may choose to wait until some other time because you want to see what happens. But this can work against you. The mere act of thinking that you have to move six months to a year from now can be very stressful.

Preparing for a Future Move

Home sellers make a lot of bad decisions when they say things like, "We are going to move in two years. What can we do to fix things up?" In most cases, they discuss this among themselves instead of consulting a professional. I always tell my clients that the moment you make that decision, just move. If you plan on moving in a year, then don't even think about fixing up anything for a year. Set a date on your calendar to discuss it with a professional, and move on with your life.

I also tell my clients that there's no need to spruce things up now if they have already decided to move two years from now. Styles will change, trends will change, and the market will change, so why spend a lot of money now making changes that may become irrelevant in two years? What if things get damaged within those two years and you have to fix them up again? It's a waste of time and money.

If you want to fix up your home for yourself, then God bless you. Do it and enjoy your home while you still live there. Go ahead and paint it some crazy color, but know that in two years, you may have to repaint it. However, if you are making changes because of resale value, then I recommend that you wait for those two years before you make that decision.

There is also the technology factor to think about. Usually, people say that they are going to move at some time in the future. They've made the decision to sell but just don't know when. With the internet, Google, and artificial intelligence that's out there, people often end up moving sooner than they thought. All of a sudden, home advertisements start popping up on your social media and news feeds. You may have settled on moving in six months, but you're probably going to start the process much earlier and move in the next month or two. That's technology at work.

There is No Perfect Season

People seem to think that it's better to sell during certain seasons of the year than others. Some sellers think that spring is a good time to list their homes. However, I cannot predict the economic factors that will be in play around spring. I must admit, though, that the majority of homes that I list do sell in the spring. But what most people don't know is that the spring market starts the day after Christmas. So, it's all about supply and demand. Just because there are more sales during this time of year doesn't mean that it's the best time to sell for you. You may have much more competition in one spring than in another.

Then there are those who think that summer is the best time to sell. Everything is green, and flowers are blooming. On the other hand, you have to consider the families with kids. Kids are out of school, vacation camps are going on, and there are many other distractions. So, there may be very little movement during summertime. In fact, if you look at the trends of when homes close, a lot of them got contracts earlier than summer but closed in the summer months.

What about winter? Isn't that the slowest season for home sales? This is what most people think. Just because one time of year has the most sales doesn't mean that it's going to be the best season for sale prices. It all depends on supply and demand. In fact, for the past five years, some of the better times to sell have been in seasons where people thought it was the worst time to sell. We're talking about around December and January.

From my experience, one of the reasons this happened is that there was a lack of properties available. Though the demand was smaller, it was still higher than the supply of available properties. So, everything I had on the market at that time that was move-in ready was sold. As you can see, sales happen in every season, and every year is different.

The most important thing is to understand the market with the help of a professional. There is a lot of misinformation that has been put out there for so many years, and people have been making the wrong decisions based on these myths. They don't have anybody to advise them, so they end up reading the information incorrectly. For example, the majority of people focus on when a property closed instead of when it went under contract. Even then, you still have to go back further and look at when the seller started to prepare the property for market. When did they start fixing it up to get the maximum amount to close in that period of time?

There's one final point that very few sellers think about. Let's say you are considering selling your home in the spring instead of right now because you think you'll make more money, but you also want to buy another property in the same general area. Let's say that your current home of $200,000 goes up in value by 5% that spring. That means you will make an extra $10,000. Well, what about that other property you want to buy? If it is valued at $500,000 at that same time frame and its value increases by the same 5%, it would be worth an extra $25,000. In other words, by waiting to buy that new your home in the spring, you will be paying that $25,000 of increased value.

Therefore, there are times when it's more beneficial to accept a lesser price for your home due to market conditions and then move into another property before it can go higher in price. It's an investment. On top of that, ask yourself where you want to live. How do you want to live your life? What kind of stress are you willing to go through just overthinking this particular decision? If you've already decided to move, just do it.

Work with a professional agent who will advise you well. There is no time like the present, so if you want to sell, do it now.

You may just end up with the best scenario possible: multiple offers. This is what we'll get into in the next chapter.

◆ ◆ ◆

I would love to set up a complimentary consultation with you! Please reach out to me through my website at www.BrianErnst. net. Also, if you would like to be connected with a wonderful agent in your area, please visit www.BrianErnst.net.

Unsure about whether you need an agent or not? Reach out, and I will personally connect you to an agent to simply have a discussion. You are still in control, and you get to decide what will work best for you!

Chapter Fourteen

The Multiple-Offer Scenario

There are a lot of problematic scenarios that can arise when selling your home. But by far, the biggest problem that you ideally want to face is receiving multiple offers for your home. How you handle this situation will determine the eventual outcome. Things can get a little tricky, so it's important that you learn how to navigate a multiple-offer scenario.

There have been situations where I received three offers and we began bidding. The home was sold over full price. However, I have also seen cases in my career where a multiple-offer situation backfired. I remember receiving three offers for a home, and I sat there thinking to myself, "I'm going to have a bidding war, and it's going to go over full price." What I didn't see coming was that all three buyers would pull out because they didn't want to be embroiled in a bidding war. This situation is a big challenge.

Juggling Multiple Offers

A bidding war is similar to juggling. If you don't know what you are doing, things can go south pretty quickly. For this reason, I never share the possibility of multiple offers with my client until the offers are officially on the table. I also don't disclose it to other agents until my client gives me permission because that's confidential information. The buyer has to commit their signed offer in writing. Then, with my client's permission, I can go ahead and share that information with the other buyers and tell them that we are in a multiple-offer situation.

At that point, I tell the buyers that the seller is requesting all parties to bring their highest and best offers to the table. Telling this to the potential buyers is not a counteroffer, which is why we can say it to everybody at the same time. I present any counteroffer that has been made by the buyers, whether written or verbal, to my seller.

This is where you need to be careful. We cannot negotiate with three different parties at the same time. Let's say that one buyer moves forward and makes a new offer for the property. We may then put a counteroffer to another interested buyer, and they may accept the counteroffer in writing. But you can't sell the home to two people! This is why a lot of these negotiations and counteroffers are kept in verbal format and not necessarily in writing. However, the initial offer should always be a written full offer that discloses all of the buyer's offer points.

The Backup Offer

As a seller, you should want a multiple-offer situation. But how it's handled can be the difference between getting a lot of money and spinning your wheels. On top of that, when you accept an offer in a multiple-offer situation, you should make sure that you have several others in waiting as backup offers.

Why is this important?

When you accept an offer, you are still waiting for the home inspection to be done. There could be home inspection issues that may come up that will determine round two of the negotiations. Some of the issues raised from a home inspection may be reasonable; for example, you might have non-functional equipment in your home. Even if these issues are expensive, they need to be addressed on any deal because in the contracts that I use, the home inspection is looking at safety and functionality concerns.

However, some of the issues raised may be unreasonable, and the buyer may ask for things that aren't appropriate. That's why in a multiple-offer situation, it's wise to hold another buyer in waiting for a short period of time in case the current offer doesn't work out. This way, you can go back and accept another offer. Keeping that other offer in waiting requires skill. Most people think that it's easy to keep a backup offer, but it isn't. You must realize that buyers aren't going to sit and wait for you. They are going to move on to the next property because they have no idea whether you are going to kill this deal or not. They don't want to wait around and get screwed over.

Keeping a potential buyer excited and waiting is not easy. In fact, it's possible that the backup offer can end up being worse than the current one that you have accepted. But you won't know that until you get out of the first deal and accept the second one. Therefore, the more information you have about the parties involved, the better. In such cases, what I'm looking for is how the buyer is purchasing the home, what their financing is, and what their terms are. If I can figure out their story and motivation behind the purchase, then we'll be in a better position. The greater the motivation the buyer has to purchase your home, the more likely they are to move. Either the deal is going to move forward, or they are probably going to be homeless or living in a hotel. Knowledge becomes power.

The multiple-offer scenario is a great one to have. But things can get a bit tricky if you aren't careful. Just make sure that you are working with an experienced agent so that you ultimately maximize the dollars in your pocket. But selecting the best offer may not be what you think. In the next chapter, you will learn what factors make up a good offer.

◆   ◆   ◆

If you would like to schedule a complimentary consultation, please visit my website at www.BrianErnst.net.

What Constitutes the Highest and Best Offer?

As a home seller, your desire is to receive the highest and best offer from a buyer. But contrary to what most people think, the highest and best offer doesn't always mean the price. It's actually about the terms of the agreement. For example, the current purchase contract that I use has 13 pages, all of which are relevant because they talk about all kinds of contingencies and additional items.

In fact, there are specific terms of the contract that may determine whether the deal is a good offer for the seller. One of these is the closing date. If the contract stipulates that the closing date is further out, it means that the seller is going to pay mortgage assessment, taxes, utilities, insurance, and liabilities on the property for a longer period of time. If it's a faster offer with a closer closing date, the seller pays less. Of course, all this will depend on what the seller's plans are for the next home they are moving into.

While one seller may want a quick closing date, another may want it pushed out quite a bit, depending on the arrangements for their next home. Therefore, the highest and best offer is not necessarily going to be about the sale price. It will involve other terms such as closing dates.

Another factor that constitutes a good offer is how the buyer wants to handle the home inspection. If a buyer agrees to buy the home as is, without bringing up anything during the home inspection, then that's a great offer. And when dealing with multiple-offer situations, the best offer is the one where the buyer agrees to pay over full price and doesn't ask for anything from the home inspection. They have decided to take a risk on the condition of the home, and this minimizes your risk of accepting that contract.

But this doesn't mean that such a deal can't go sideways. You're just minimizing risk. Therefore, though the highest and best price is important, it also depends on how you get to that price with those terms and in your current situation. It's all dependent on each offer, the way the buyer is paying for the property, and the likelihood that their financing will go through.

As I said before, there are 13 pages in my current purchase contract, so there are a lot of different things to consider. At the end of the day, the highest and best offer is the best combination of price, timing, and terms.

Chapter Sixteen

The Guaranteed Sale Program

A guaranteed sale program is when a seller agrees to have their home listed for sale, and if the agent cannot sell it, the real estate company buys it from the seller. Technically, it is a guarantee that somebody will buy your home within an agreed period of time.

But wait! There's a catch...

The challenge of guaranteed sale programs is the actual price that you end up with. If you look at relocation companies, you will discover that most of them have packages that involve a guaranteed sale. If they cannot sell the home within a set period of time, the relocation company will buy it from you at a certain price. This price is typically lower that what most sellers think their home is worth. The only way to know for sure is to try it out.

So, why would a seller agree to this?

Well, this is a good deal for those sellers who are in a time crunch and want to move as quickly as possible. I have witnessed this on quite a number of relocations. The seller couldn't get the price they wanted and accepted the price offer from the relocation company just to get on with their move. This doesn't necessarily mean that the home is out of the seller's hands at that point. Sometimes, an agent is still involved.

Gimmick or Lifeline?

One thing you need to understand is that real estate agents who provide guaranteed sale programs are typically going to offer it just to get in your door. It's an advertising strategy, and their main agenda is to get in the door and meet you. Then, they'll tell you about their guaranteed sale programs and present you with their terms.

These terms may include as many as 30 requirements that you have to abide by for the guaranteed sale. For example, you have to be available to show your home for a specific amount of time for seven days a week. You have to price your home for a certain percentage under its market value so as to get more people through the door and attract more offers. You will basically be underpricing your property to fit into the given time frame.

By the way, I'm not afraid of underpricing your property because I know I will sell it for that much over the list price. But in my experience, most people don't believe that buyers will pay over list price. There are some years when I'll have as many as a third of my listings selling at full price or above. During certain times of the year, I'll have half my listings sell at full price or above. Most people I have worked with through the years don't think this way.

The guaranteed sale program basically tells you everything that you need to do to sell your home within a certain period of time, all so that the real estate agent will not have to buy it from you. If the agent does buy it, then they will do it so much under market value that it will make sense for them.

I know quite a few agents who do offer guaranteed sales programs, but very few sellers actually sign up for it. The reason is that when most home sellers see the terms required for such a program, they balk at it. Since the biggest factor is pricing, you need to price it aggressively to sell quickly. However, these programs can be helpful because they show you the terms and best practices to abide by to sell your home quickly.

The contingent price that the agent or their company will offer is going to be advantageous to them. They know they can flip the home and sell it for profit in the short term. Therefore, you need to ask yourself whether it is a good deal for you. For those sellers who are in a big rush to move, it may be useful to sign up for a guaranteed sales program. But for the majority of sellers, this may not be a good idea. You should go ahead and take a look at the requirements spelled out, but just know that it isn't necessarily going to maximize what you get from the deal.

In the next chapter, you will learn how to properly prepare for a home inspection.

Chapter Seventeen

Preparing for a Home Inspection

Before you prepare for any home inspection, you must first understand how it works and what it entails.

A home inspection usually happens once the buyer and seller agree to terms. The contract terms actually specify the number of days within which a home inspection has to be performed, which in most cases, is within the first week or so of a property going under contract. This is something that must be undertaken by a licensed professional or home inspector, not your dad's roommate from college or some plumber friend.

The home inspector will look at the property and try to find any safety and functionality concerns. Though they may bring up other cosmetic issues, most of the contracts I use focus primarily on safety and functionality concerns. Period. If such issues are discovered, the buyer may ask the seller to repair them or provide a credit.

That's the nature of round table negotiations. But what happens when the buyer wants some things fixed and the seller refuses to repair anything? Well, that will depend on how badly the buyer wants the property. The buyer can decide to acquire the home and fix it later.

Beware of Legal and Contractual Issues

It is also important to understand that the practice of law and actual law are two different things. There are a number of instances where people have tried to use the home inspection as leverage during a negotiation. I have seen cases where the buyer seeks to negotiate based on issues that they are not contractually supposed to ask for.

For example, I recently had a situation where I had an as-is contract. The buyer decided to get a home inspection done anyway, which is within their rights, but they then asked us to fix numerous issues that weren't even wrong with the property. We went ahead and offered them a credit for those items, but they refused to take it. When we hired professional inspectors to come in and take a look, they reported that there was nothing broken. This was a weird situation because they legally and contractually should never have brought up these issues under an as-is contract. The seller had the right to take up legal action against the buyer. We were still in the negotiation stage, so the seller hadn't really lost anything at that point. Despite the fact that they had messed with the law, there was no actual quantifiable loss. We also had to consider the costs of taking them to court. Maybe we would have lost. I'm not an attorney, so I don't know these things, which is why you need to align yourself with the right people who know how to get through these problems. The practice of law and actual written law are completely different, and I have seen many people out there take advantage of this.

Can a buyer use a home inspection as a way to get out of a contract?

Of course they can! But this will depend on the type of contract they are in. With the contract I use, the buyer is allowed to get out within the first five business days, but with my current home inspection contract, it now goes through 10 days to negotiate that out. So, if they really want to get out of the contract, there is a way to do that. The buyer can have unreasonable requests, and when the seller refuses, the buyer can walk away.

My home inspection contract, however, is designed for more. If the buyer raises an issue with safety and functionality problems that make the home uninhabitable and the seller doesn't address them, then they can walk away. That's really the intent of it. Sometimes, people just want to get out of a contract, so they make ridiculous requests and use that as an excuse to walk away.

How to Prepare for the Inspection

One of the questions I keep getting from my clients is, "Should I perform a home inspection ahead of time?" Usually, they have read something on the internet, and they think it would be a good idea to get their own inspector to check the home first. Though this may be a great idea in theory, it doesn't make much financial sense.

Let me tell you why.

A home inspector is trained to find problems. If you hire three different home inspectors, they will present you with a list of problems. However, the problems they find will not be exactly the same. I know this for a fact because I have had the same properties checked with multiple inspectors, and every home inspector found something different.

Your home inspector may bring up an issue that the buyer's home inspector will never discover. Do you want to risk that? Why waste money to pay somebody to find something that the buyer's home inspector may never find? I would recommend that you instead fix the cosmetic and functionality issues that you already know need to be addressed. Don't go sniffing around for all kinds of problems.

Just like when you are selling a used car, you should focus on washing it, cleaning it to remove all the little rocks and pebbles from the clear coat, waxing it, and buffing it, then adding another layer of wax after that. On top of that, you can clean the interior and make it perfectly shiny. Most people don't look under the hood of cars anyway, so if you decide to wash the inside of the hood, you may needlessly damage the engine and other parts in there. A lot of people mess up their cars by cleaning under the hood with a power spray. So, stick to fixing the cosmetic stuff, but don't bring in someone to dig around your furnace unless you know the furnace isn't working.

Imagine if you spent time and money to get someone to mess around in your furnace. Let's say it takes you weeks to get a spare part for something. But then the buyer comes up and says that they will buy the home as-is, with no home inspection needed. Think of how silly you will feel wasting all that money and time on something that was unnecessary.

Another point I would like to make is that paying for your own home inspection is a waste of time. As the seller, you should be busy getting your home out on the market. Imagine having a home inspection, fixing up all those issues that were raised, and then, the buyer's home inspector still finds problems that the first inspector didn't. You will be wasting both time and money addressing additional issues. You may have even wasted time and money fixing problems that the buyer's home inspector would never have found.

Let's look at it another way. If the buyer's home inspector finds something, you and the buyer can negotiate a credit to address those issues. You may end up realizing that the credit is not as expensive as the cost of repairs that you would have done yourself. You just never know.

At the end of the day, it pays to be patient and let the buyer's home inspector go through your home and find whatever issues they discover. Then, you can address those issues afterward either by repairing the problems or negotiating some sort of credit with the buyer. This is a better strategy than second-guessing what the inspector is going to find and second-guessing what the buyer will want addressed.

Just handle the issues with your home specifically during the home inspection period. Be prepared and budget for some issues as well. When it comes to getting an inspection ahead of time, it may be ideal only if you have an older home that has quite a few issues in it. This is especially true in situations where you have non-visible issues that you don't know about.

If there are issues that are out in the open like faulty switches, outlets, and appliances, then go ahead and get them fixed. You have been living in the property, so you should be aware of these problems. But if you haven't lived in the property, then go ahead and test everything out to make sure it works.

Work on things like carpeting, flooring, and painting, and then go to the appliances and fixtures. Flooring and painting offer the biggest return on investment by far if repaired ahead of time. Focus on things that are either broken or so outdated that potential buyers won't accept them. This way, your home will be ready for viewing during the open home.

◆ ◆ ◆

I would love to set up a complimentary consultation with you! Please reach out to me through my website at www.BrianErnst.net. Also, if you would like to be connected with a wonderful agent in your area, please visit www.BrianErnst.net.

Unsure about whether you need an agent or not? Reach out, and I will personally connect you to an agent to simply have a discussion. You are still in control, and you get to decide what will work best for you!

Chapter Eighteen

How to Handle Open Houses

Part of selling a home is enabling potential buyers to view the property before deciding on whether to purchase or not. This is why we always have an open house. It is an effective way of showing your home and attracting buyers. Let's look at the different types of open houses.

Types of Open Houses

There are generally two types of open houses. There's the public open house and the broker open house. You are probably familiar with the first category, where anyone can walk in and see the home. However, a broker open house is where your agent or broker holds an open house for other agents and brokers. Personally, I am not a big fan of broker open houses because I don't have the time to go and preview properties. I just don't see the point of this kind of open house.

I know many brokers who love broker open houses because it's a great way to connect with other agents. In fact, most of the agents I know have never previewed properties before they've actually brought their clients in. The agents who go to broker open houses are clearly not working with qualified buyers. If they were, they would just go with their buyer and show them the property. Gaining access to these properties is easy for the most part. If it's a very exclusive property, then that's another story, and that's when a broker open house would make more sense. Properties that are more upscale and very exclusive can have a broker open house because it's for a limited audience. But the home will sell either way because it's still listed on the MLS and any agent can find it.

The thing that I don't want is for some agent down the street who has a listed property to come to my broker open house, look at it, and go back to use that information to adjust their price and become our competition. They may go and tell their client to lower their sale price because the home they just looked at is going for much less. I don't want this to happen. Of course, the same thing can happen in a public open house. The neighbors who have listed their homes down the street may come and look at the open house to compare prices. This is a possibility. However, most sellers just don't have the guts to do such a thing. They really don't.

With public open houses, you generally have a better chance of winning the lottery than selling the property during the actual open house. In most cases, open houses work to motivate a buyer who has seen the property during the week and is afraid that it will sell during one of the open houses on the weekend. It is a motivational factor for buyers.

Benefits of an Open House

Lazy agents can actually take advantage of an open house by sending their clients to the property without actually showing it to them. I see this happen on a regular basis. The next thing you know, Monday comes along, and we get an offer even before that lazy agent has had the chance to set up an appointment.

One of the biggest benefits of an open house to a seller comes with working with an experienced agent. If you hire an experienced agent who consistently does open houses in your area, they will know what the public is looking for, what the current market is like, and what's going on with the current pulse of the area. In fact, it could be a previous open house that helps sell their current listing.

Therefore, open houses are beneficial to both the seller and the agent. It's a great way to show and give the public access to your home, but it can also help the agent sell their other listings. If a buyer doesn't want to buy my current listing, then I can sell them something else in my listing. An agent who is consistently doing open houses will have that pulse of the area and, hopefully, acquire the contacts of potential buyers and agents who come through and make solid purchase offers.

If I have a listing of quite a few properties and tend to know which agents have buyers who are seeking certain types of properties, I often pick up the phone and call them to say, "Hey, this is what I've got." Sometimes, they reach out to me and ask me for tips about properties in certain neighborhoods because they know I always have something coming up. They tell me what they are looking for, and I check my listing. In specific neighborhoods, I'll have a private listing where the properties are not even active on the MLS. I'll make a couple of phone calls and get three offers really easily.

As you can see, open houses are very advantageous to agents because good agents are not looking for buyers; they are looking for other sellers during an open house. That's what a good agent will do. They want the nosy neighbors so that they can sell them homes. With the access and type of marketing I do for open houses, my properties are often exposed to more people than an average open house. As a result, these open houses are also more helpful for sellers.

The Broker Tour Gimmick

A broker tour is where a listing agent brings a group of brokers to a seller's home. It is a selling point for listing agents to tell their clients: "Look, I can bring 30 brokers through your property right away." Unfortunately, statistics show that most agents don't sell a lot of properties. Therefore, it doesn't mean that those 30 brokers will translate into an avalanche of potential buyers.

On my board of realtors last year, 71% of the 18,000 agents closed zero or just one transaction in a year. That shows you that these brokers have a lot of time on their hands, and it's easy for that particular brokerage to gather 30 people to come through your home. A broker tour doesn't mean they have any buyers with them. They are just trying to make a selling point to the seller (you) that they managed to bring a lot of people through. It is deceptive and doesn't equate to results.

I want to deal with qualified buyers on my listings. I don't have a single listing that an agent cannot schedule an appointment for on any day of the week. If an agent has a qualified buyer, they won't waste time with broker tours. They will use their access to my listings to set up an appointment to see the property. A broker open house only makes sense if the seller is very particular about how people come through the property. But of course, this would be a very bad thing because it would limit the number of people who come through the property.

Ultimately, the broker tour is a sales gimmick that helps the real estate agent secure the listing from the home seller. It isn't very beneficial to the actual sale of the home.

Chapter Nineteen

Photography and Videography of Your Home

In Chapter 8, I mentioned how videos and photography can be used as part of the marketing strategy to sell your home. Therefore, it is important to understand what kind of video or photography is needed to get the job done well. There are some factors that must be considered when handling this type of marketing strategy.

Too Much Information Can Hurt You

Though good photography and video are crucial for marketing purposes, photos that are too good might show off more flaws than necessary. This may limit the number of people who come to view the property. The goal is to get them to come to the property so that they can develop a stronger emotional attachment to it. This is something that isn't easy to do online.

My job is to get qualified people through the door of my listed properties. If I give them too much information, they won't need to come in because they can either rule it in or rule it out depending on what they see. Therefore, I always use professional photographers and videographers for my listings. I should also tell you that for 13 years of my career, I was a professional photographer. I have 13 years of photography experience, but most people who don't know this think that I have no clue what I'm doing. No, I was taking photos myself and editing them. Now that technology has become advanced, I don't have the same amount of time to edit them as I used to. You need to work with experienced agents. They will delegate the process to a professional and focus on what they do best: selling more homes and advising their sellers. I use professional photographers and adjust the package I purchase depending on the type of listing I have.

What Type of Property Do You Have?

Something you should be aware of is that the type of home you're selling is a major factor in the type of photography and video you'll want to use. If I have a $2 million listing in an area where the average sale price is about $400,000 or less, I am going to go crazy on the photography and videography. I am going to spend a lot of money on high-quality pictures so that when you look out the window in the photo, you can clearly see the high-quality surroundings. I don't want to get too technical on this, but I do not do this with less expensive properties. I don't want people to look out the windows and see an unattractive view. So, for the less expensive properties, I don't take high-quality photos.

When it comes to videos, I try not to show everything in the property. There are types of virtual tours that we can use, such as Matterport videos. This involves taking a 3D video of the floor plan of the property so that you can twist it around to show people what it looks like from the outside. You can show people what the home would look like if the walls were removed. You can also use it to show what the home would look like with the furniture in place but no walls or floors.

Though it's a very interesting process, it is quite expensive. Thus, we don't use it for certain properties because it would be a waste; for example, properties that are too small to really show off. But when dealing with large, high-end properties, Matterport video tours help to show it all off. I want to show every functionality of the home, such as the theater, bar, spa, and the large walk-in closet that is bigger than most people's second floor.

Therefore, these are the types of things that are considered in different markets and for different types of properties. Most of the typical homes that people live in are not displayed using very high-quality images, and we avoid using a camera angle that shows too much. Things may get distorted, and a room that is 12 by 12 may end up looking like it's 20 by 20. It may look attractive to buyers when they see the photos, but they'll be really angry when they see the actual thing. There are times when pictures can seem deceptive, so it's a balance of adequately showing off the home without overexposing it and all its flaws. We also have to be careful not to show too little so that people aren't interested enough.

About 15 years ago, we would put as few as three pictures on the MLS. We would have the main picture, the outside picture, and two really good interior photos. Then, we would have different links to our website so that we would capture interested buyers ourselves. Technology has come so far that we can't do that anymore. Today, if you don't give people everything, they will simply skip it and move on to the next property. People expect that they will be able to see all the pictures they want immediately.

Chapter Twenty

Selling a Home by Yourself

It may have crossed your mind at some point to sell your home by yourself without involving the services of a professional real estate agent. If this is the route that you choose to go, then there are some crucial things you need to consider.

Time, Money, and Effort

The first points of comparison here are the money and the time factors. Statistically speaking, selling your home via a licensed real estate agent is much faster and will get you more money than when you do it yourself. With For Sale By Owner homes, most sellers typically get anywhere from 7% to 11% less than they would if they were represented by an agent. When you factor in a commission, then a lot of times, the figures are much less than that.

Something else to know is that when you choose For Sale By Owner, the buyer's pool is composed of people who want to save money. Therefore, they are likely to offer you much less because they know you aren't paying a commission to an agent. This is why you are likely to get a much lower price on average. You can either pay a commission to the buyer or pay it to an agent who will do all the work.

Do you have the necessary experience to do all the work and get through the deal from start to finish?

You may think you are saving on that agent commission, but you will quickly realize that you only have a small pool of buyers to deal with. I'm not trying to discourage you or force you to get an agent. It is absolutely possible to sell your home on your own. But agents exist because there is a demand for our services. I have spent my whole career learning how to do this in the most efficient and effective way that puts the most money in my client's pocket.

Using an agent is simply a lot less stressful, and the better their experience and track record, the better the results for you. You have to ask yourself how quickly you want to sell your home and whether you want to maximize your return on your investment.

Sale by Owner vs. Sale by Agent

So, what are some of the reasons why selling by owner may not be a good idea?

1. **Too many people to negotiate with.** If you will be handling everything yourself, then be prepared to negotiate with the buyer, the buyer's agent, the buyer's attorney, the home inspection companies, and in some cases, the appraiser. Every single one of these people are looking out for the buyer's best interest to get them the best deal possible. All these people are working against you as the seller, and you barely have any experience to adequately negotiate with them.

2. **Exposure to prospective purchasers.** There are studies that show that more than 88% of buyers search for a home online, and that's in the upper 90% by today's statistics. Therefore, there is a very small fraction of buyers who are looking for homes that are for sale by owner.

3. **Exposure to internet marketing.** Real estate agents have greater access to marketing tools and systems that can boost the exposure of your home on many platforms. The days of planting a sign in the front yard and placing an ad in the paper are long gone.

4. **Paperwork and regulations.** Nowadays, there is tons of paperwork that you have to contend with when selling and buying a home. The industry has dramatically increased the amount of paperwork, disclosures, and regulations that sellers have to deal with. This has led to a massive decrease in the number of properties that are for sale by owner over the last 20 years. Most sellers are not familiar with all the different regulations, and this can ultimately lead to a failed deal.

5. **Return on investment.** As I said before, you will get more money when using a licensed real estate agent than when selling your home yourself. I'm talking about an agent licensed with the National Realtor Association, not just someone who is super experienced. There's a 7% to 11% difference in price, which is quite significant.

Do you still want to go through the entire process yourself?

For these reasons, I recommend that you talk to an experienced real estate professional and see what they have to offer. One of the questions that I ask FSBO (for sale by owner) sellers when I come across them is this: If a buyer came in today and said they would give you the price you want, would you take the deal? Almost every FSBO seller that I've talked to replies with a yes. What they don't realize is that just because a buyer agrees to buy at your price doesn't mean they qualify to buy at that price. Follow up questions would be: Do you know when and how to find out if they are qualified? What about all the time and energy you will have wasted? What if the market shifts and you are now left in a worse situation, with a ridiculously overpriced home that nobody is looking at?

Let me try to put make this more clear. When you really think about it, you are sacrificing a great deal to go along the for sale by owner route. You may think that you are saving money on the realtor commission, but the truth is that you are actually sacrificing money both in the sale price and the various parts of the negotiation. A realtor can help you through those negotiations to make sure that you are getting the best possible result out of the sale of your home. That realtor is also there to represent your best interests against the opposing agent and buyer, who only have their own interests at heart. That's the reality of it.

Let me end by saying this:

A good real estate agent has such an incredible value for the seller of the home. Here's a final statistic to prove it. In a survey, of all the people who opted to sell their homes via a for sale by owner route, 90% of them stated that they would list their home with a realtor if they had to sell their home again. That is a reflection of the experience that they had to go through. That tells you that such a large percentage of people who went through that solo process would never do it that way again.

Lesson learned!

◆　◆　◆

If you would like to schedule a complimentary consultation, please visit my website at www.BrianErnst.net.

Chapter Twenty One

Finding the Best Real Estate Agent

Now that we have settled the issue of why you need to work with an agent vs. selling the home yourself, let's look at where and how to find the best agent. There are certain criteria that you need to focus on when doing your search.

Sources of Real Estate Agents

There are a number of different sources that can help you find good real estate agents:

1. **Local advertisements:** For one, it depends on how long you have lived in or owned the property. In other words, how well do you know what's going on in the area? Is there a specific agent who's been advertising in your neighborhood for years? This could be through the mail, flyers, email, billboards, or even shopping carts at the grocery store. Whatever it is, do you see an agent that is advertising in your area and the homes that they actually sell? You can also look at the number of signs that you see in your neighborhood. Is there a specific agent who has dominated the area, selling homes through the years? Not just listing properties *but actually selling them.* Look for an agent who put the sold sign on a property rather than one who simply put up their sign for 12 months.

2. **Online resources:** There are some websites that you can use for specific areas, but these websites are constantly changing, so it's difficult to say which ones are best. However, Zillow is a good example of one. Ideally, you should be searching these websites for agents who are the top producers in that area.

3. **Referrals:** Another way to find agents is by asking people for referrals in the area. Don't just accept a referral because the agent is somebody's friend's brother who happens to be in real estate type of stuff. Look for a person who everybody knows as the expert in the area.

Criteria for Selecting an Agent

The first criterion to use is the amount and type of experience an agent has. Just because someone has been licensed for 30 years doesn't mean they know what they are doing. I may be working with someone who has been in the business for a short period of time but they are very aggressive, in tune with the market, and knowledgeable about the marketing that needs to be done. Very often, you will find real estate agents who are behind the times when it comes to technology. So, there are times when someone who is new to the industry and has learned these newer technologies may actually be better than an agent who has been licensed for 30 years but doesn't have a lot of transactions or has lost their passion and drive.

It's tempting to try to find the agents who have sold the most homes, but that is not necessarily the best approach. You should make sure that you find someone who offers the best services and has the best success in selling within your specific area. This is the kind of agent who will give you the best advice on selling your home.

You should also look at which agent sells homes the fastest. This is something you need to think about ahead of time because once you decide to hire an agent, it is usually too late. You will probably go with the first person someone recommended or the first person that pops up. This might end up being the wrong person. So, think about this in advance.

An agent with local knowledge and expertise is a great asset. Whenever I sold homes in different states with other real estate agents, I often knew as much or more than the average local agent. However, there are certain aspects of the local area that I didn't know about, so the expert agent I partnered with would answer whatever questions I had. I may not have liked the answer, but at least I understood it, and we moved forward. I recommend that you work with an agent who has done enough business in that area.

If the agent is really good, then they don't necessarily have to be from that area. In the industry today, the majority of real estate advertising is online, which means agents can broaden their areas of influence. There are some great agents who cover a broad area and can do a great job because they have closed more transactions. Therefore, as an agent, being hyper-local doesn't always work exactly the way it used to, say, 20 or 30 years ago. It's helpful, but when an agent is too focused on a small area, they will have blinders on and won't see the broader market. This kind of agent won't be able to tell a seller whether the overall market is dropping so that they can adjust the price to catch up to the market. By the time they realize what's happening, it may be too late.

Personality is also a key factor because it will determine your working relationship. I would advise that you talk to different agents to see who they are, what they are like, and how they express their personalities. Ideally, you want to work with someone who is a good fit for you. Find out what services they provide so that you are always on the same page.

As a real estate agent, when I work with another agent, I approach the pricing issue differently. I've done this for a long time, and I understand that when it comes to pricing, it's not the agent's pricing that is important. It's about the pricing that I decide and how they present their thoughts on that pricing. I try to find out the depth of information they have that I may not have. Though so much stuff is in the public domain today thanks to technology, it is no substitute for the experience that comes with selling so many properties. Doing a lot of deals really provides a whole different perspective. For this reason, I talk to quite a few agents if I need to.

Due to my experience and knowledge, I generally know who is an expert agent in a certain locale. So, when I pick up the phone, I'm just calling one person because I have already vetted various agents for particular areas over the years. I already know how good they are and the results they have achieved because I pay attention to such things. All I need to know is whether they are available. Therefore, I recommend that all homeowners pay attention to this every so often. There's no need to take three hours a week to do this. Just pay attention when you see some advertisements or a mailer from somebody. Store or save things like that so that when you need an agent, you can simply take a look at who's been reaching out to you.

Dealing with a Team of Agents

It is possible that you may end up dealing with a team setup where you have multiple agents working to sell your property. This is a good scenario for a seller. However, you have to understand and clarify how your communication channels will flow. Who will be your main point of contact when it comes to talking to the real estate agent? Who will you be working with? What is the communication process to be used? You need to clarify these things early on.

You may not be dealing directly with the head agent and may be assigned a different one. As long as you understand how the process is structured and how the team works, then it's okay. Sometimes, those agents that are big and do a lot of transactions have many other resources available. They are advertising many properties, and one of their other listings can actually help to sell your home. If one of the properties is under contract and your listing is not, more people can be steered toward your property just because of that advertisement source from that bigger agent.

Using My Services

If you are looking to work directly with me or want access to my network of agents, then I would be glad to help. It doesn't matter whether you live in Illinois (where I reside) or another state. I have a huge referral network all across the country and even internationally as well. I would be happy to vet a real estate agent for you; that is, if I don't already have one for you. Of course, this will depend specifically on what you are looking for and other details.

I have done this for years and interviewed so many agents for my clients who were moving to different states. Therefore, it is crucial for me to make sure that I set you up with the best person for the job by interviewing them personally on your behalf. Then, I provide you with the agent and the area they work in, according to what you are looking for. They will also have some of the exact properties and listings that fit your criteria, so they are more likely to know what you are looking for. Different real estate companies have different styles of operation, and different brokerages have different ways of doing things. Due to my vast experience, I can usually tell which ones are which. This is the basic idea of it. Let an experienced professional help you find an experienced professional. I am happy to do that if you want me to help you find an agent.

It may take a bit of time for me to find the right person for you, but sometimes, it doesn't. I had an instance where this happened recently. One of my clients was moving to Indianapolis, and he didn't really want me to set him up with an agent because he was already working with one in Indianapolis. His wife was already in Indianapolis, staying in some rental property, so they were working with an agent to look for a new home. I told him that his decision was fine with me but that if he ever needed something, he should let me know. I said that if he needed an agent, something went sideways, or whatever situation came up, he shouldn't hesitate to reach out to me.

So, I went ahead and sold his home. After I had closed on his property and he had moved to Indiana, he called me out of the blue and said, "Brian, I know you told me before that you have some people or you can set me up with some people. Can you help me out? The agent we were working with in Indianapolis is not working out. We are having problems with several things." It sounded to me like they were having legitimate problems, so I told him that I would call him back in five minutes. I already knew exactly who to call. I made one phone call to an agent. I told them that I had a past client who was in the middle of some problem and explained what it was all about. I asked the agent to reach out to my client in about 10 minutes because I wanted to call him first to inform him about the new agent's name. The agent agreed, and I called my client back. I told him, "I just reached out to a real estate agent, and she's an incredible agent who knows what she's doing. She has a lot of experience and is incredibly good at helping people find exactly what they are looking for." By the end of the following weekend, he was under contract with another property, and it closed.

It is just that easy when you set them up with the right people. It was done quickly, and that was it. It was fantastic. I love having referral partners that can take care of my clients because I know I can refer clients to them and trust excellent results will follow. I think that's the most important thing because my reputation is at stake. When clients are trusting in me and I'm handing them off to someone else, I know that those people are going to take responsibility and fix issues in case anything gets screwed up. If things go well, they can take the credit. That's what needs to be done.

People are not perfect, but how they handle the imperfections and mistakes of life is a big factor in every transaction. There are so many people involved in a real estate transaction, and you can't necessarily pinpoint one person or another when it comes to who needs to take responsibility. We are dealing with a lot of personalities during a transaction, not just the two agents, the buyer, and the seller. In most cases, we are dealing with probably more than 20 people who are actually touching a single deal.

Who are these people? We have attorneys, attorney staff on both sides depending on each state, the title company, their staff, and mortgage companies. Then there's appraisers, home inspectors, surveyors, etc. Most people don't even realize just how many people are involved in a single real estate transaction. Any one of these people involved in a deal can mess it up.

That's why I will always hand off specific issues with a transaction to a person who I know is a problem solver. Problems do happen, so if something comes up, these people will fix it.

◆ ◆ ◆

I would love to set up a complimentary consultation with you! Please reach out to me through my website at www.BrianErnst.net. Also, if you would like to be connected with a wonderful agent or lender in your area, please visit www.BrianErnst.net.

Unsure about whether you need an agent or lender? Reach out, and I will personally connect you with one to simply have a discussion. You are still in control, and you get to decide what will work best for you!

Chapter Twenty Two

Using a Family Member or Friend to List Your Home

Sometimes, a homeowner may have a family member or friend who happens to be a real estate agent. Obviously, when they decide to sell their home, they would think of listing it with them because they already know them very well. But is listing your home with a friend or family member a good idea?

Before I answer this question, let me give you a bit of my background.

I have been in real estate for quite a long time. In fact, I come from a family of real estate agents. My grandmother was a real estate agent. She got my cousin, who is like an uncle to me, into real estate. He then got me into real estate, and I worked for 14 years in his office as a manager. Therefore, we have quite a bit of real estate experience in our family.

Now, would I recommend that you go to your family member, maybe your Uncle Bob who has done two deals here and there and works another job? No, I wouldn't encourage you to do that. There are two reasons why I say this.

The first has to do with experience. Uncle Bob may have closed two deals, but how much experience does he have? The second is terminating their services. If they cannot get the deal done, how awkward is it going to be when you are forced to fire them? There you are, dealing with one of the biggest investments in your life, and your family member is failing you. Firing a family member or a friend is a lot harder to do than firing somebody who you don't know personally. Therefore, you need to consider their track record, their experience level, and their ability to separate their emotions from their professional responsibility. They will have to be dispassionate when giving advice to you, as it could be as uncomfortable for them to discuss difficult aspects about selling your home.

Getting Emotionally Involved

From my experience, when I give out advice and I am too emotionally involved in it, it often affects the deal negatively. I may unconsciously hurt the situation. That's why I do my best to be dispassionate and try to be a neutral third party to make sure I give my clients the best advice. Being neutral doesn't mean I am not representing my client's best interests. I do represent them and have a vested interest in their happiness and success. But at the end of the day, I have to take a step back far enough away to see the bigger picture.

In fact, this happened to me recently. One of my clients told me that they didn't want to agree to some of the home inspection issues. I can't remember all the details about the home inspection report, but I recall that we were about $1,000 apart. That is $1,000 apart on a $300,000 home that we had already negotiated the contract for. All that remained was to just negotiate the home inspection issues.

So, I told my client, "Let's look at this situation here. I agree with you that the price that you are selling your home for plus the concessions you are making are probably unfair. But let's talk a little more about this situation. The market has shifted at the moment, and I don't know when I can get a contract on your home again. It's currently vacant, yet you are paying the mortgage, assessments, taxes, utilities, and insurance every single month. I don't know whether I can get showings. It's probably going to take me about three months to get another contract because the market is really slow right now. So, if it takes three months for a contract and 45 days to close, that means we have a long way to go. How much are you paying in mortgage, taxes, utilities, assessment, and insurance? A lot of things could happen to a vacant property because there's nobody in there. We may not find out about an issue until after the fact, so that's high risk. If you compare the $1,000 bucks to the months and months of expenses you will be paying, it makes more financial sense to give up a little bit more money now. How are you going to feel down the road if I am unable to sell the home anytime soon? What if the market shifts and goes lower? You would find yourself in a worse situation. I would rather wrap it up with a bow and be done with it."

For those homeowners who don't have mortgages on their properties, they may not feel the same measure of anxiety as those who do. But those mortgage payments are like cash that's sitting in the property going nowhere. You can put that money toward something else if you choose not to buy another home or investment. If you feel like you didn't make enough money on the result of the transaction or the sale of your property, go invest it somewhere else to make up for it. Don't sit on it for months, hoping and waiting to sell your home. It could take another six months before we get the home under contract, and we may still end up facing the same problems or even worse. If you are working with a friend or family member, they may be too emotionally invested in your deal to make a rational decision like this.

So, would I use friends and family to sell my home? It all depends on their experience and how they will handle the process, especially when problems arise. Don't forget that it's hard to fire someone you know well or are related to. You will still be related to your family member, but they may not be your friend after that.

Would you invite Uncle Bob over for Thanksgiving dinner to spend time in the very same home that you fired him over?

Think about that!

Conclusion

Selling your home quickly and for top dollar requires you to effectively crack the home seller's code. This book has taken you on a journey of discovering how the real estate industry works from an insider's perspective. Now, you have a better understanding of how to go about it and what to expect when selling your home.

You have learned the factors that determine the pricing of a property and the costs that are typically incurred by both parties. I also explained where to find a real estate agent, how to hire the best person for the job, and what to expect from them. Of all the recommendations that I provided in the book, this BY FAR is the most important one. Working with the right agent will determine how the transactions move and whether you will walk away happy or disgruntled. Take this advice very seriously.

I also explained how to stage and prepare your home for potential buyers so that your home sells faster and for as much money as possible. There may be a lot of factors that are outside of your control. However, you should now understand just how much power your own decisions can have on the deal. Your choice of agent, deciding to sell your home yourself, involving yourself in the marketing, or preparing your home for inspection: These are just some of the decisions that can make or break a deal. That's why you need an experienced and professional agent who can properly guide you every step of the way.

I know that it is impossible to cover everything in one book. There are many nitty gritty details about home-selling that may not have been discussed. However, I know that the information you have learned here is going to be extremely invaluable to you as you sell your home in the future. I have done my best to leverage my 16+ years of real estate experience to provide you with answers to some of the most pertinent and common questions that home sellers ask. I hope you find this information valuable and make use of it. Just having knowledge is not power. The power is in the application of that knowledge.

Use it or lose it.

◆　◆　◆

I would love to set up a complimentary consultation with you! Please reach out to me through my website at www.BrianErnst.net. Also, if you would like to be connected with a wonderful agent in your area, please visit www.BrianErnst.net.

Unsure about whether you need an agent or not? Reach out, and I will personally connect you to an agent to simply have a discussion. You are still in control, and you get to decide what will work best for you!

Review Inquiry

Hey, it's Brian Ernst here, and I'm the book's author.

I hope you've enjoyed the book, finding it both useful and fun. **I have a favor to ask you. Would you consider giving it a rating on Amazon, please?** One way to help establish the book's status is with a boat-load of Amazon love that speaks to why its valued. If you found value in this book, please consider leaving an honest review!

Many thanks in advance,

Brian Ernst

About the Author

Brian Ernst has over 16 years of real estate experience, making him one of the top-producing agents in Illinois. As CEO of the Brian Ernst Realty Group, he successfully manages a $30+ million-a-year production team. Brian uses state-of-the-art systems and best-in-class processes that ensure his clients get what they want and need. Utilizing his real estate expertise, Brian is also a motivational speaker, group coach, mastermind facilitator, and a consultant.

Brian believes in the importance of being in a constant state of learning and developing professionally. His ability to apply his "growth" mindset has translated into outstanding results for his clients. Brian has managed and coached agents nationally to achieve up to a 400% improvement to their businesses. He also presents hundreds of free workshops to help any individuals who want to accelerate their success.

Brian attended Indiana University, Western Illinois University, and Benedictine University for business management and MBA studies.

Brian Ernst can be reached at: https://www.brianernst.net/

Made in the USA
Lexington, KY
16 November 2019